The Final Decade: the 1960s Steam Railway

Images from the Paul Hocquard collection at The Transport Treasury
Selected by Kevin Robertson

© Images and design: The Transport Treasury 2021. Text Kevin Robertson

ISBN 978-1-913893-04-0

First Published in 2021 by Transport Treasury Publishing Ltd. 16 Highworth Close, High Wycombe, HP13 7PJ

Totem Publishing, an imprint of Transport Treasury Publishing.

www.ttpublishing.co.uk

Printed in Malta by Gutenberg Press.

'The Final Decade: the 1960s Steam Railway' is one of a series of books on specialist transport subjects published in strictly limited numbers and produced under the Totem Publishing imprint using material only available at The Transport Treasury.

Front cover: (1) The *attraction* of steam. It may be a cold day, it may be the carriage was a lot more appealing, but the engine, the train, the atmosphere oozes the steam railway. Generations of boys (and men), and sometimes girls too, would stand riveted to the spot, just to be absorbed in the atmosphere. To the railwaymen themselves whether that be on the platform, in the offices, or on the engine, it was a job, secure and safe, that is until wholesale line closures, amalgamations and general modernisation took place. Once there had been a true pride in the job, now it was 'leave whilst there is the chance of something else or just keep your head down'.

Frontispiece: (2) The unmistakable outline of a Great Western 'Castle' at Wolverhampton. Opposite, a memory of the past when the railways were the common carrier of parcels - shopping by post is certainly not a trait of the modern generation. British Railways would slowly move away from parcels and it would all end with Red Star in the days of privatisation. Years before that all the members of the 'Castle' class had been withdrawn from service and now it is electric trains that operate between Wolverhampton and London.

Rear cover: (104) It is easy to forget the time when freight was the mainstay of railway operation. Main line freight of all sorts, although without doubt coal for both industry and domestic use was the dominant product carried for many years. Indeed, most stations had a coal yard but all are now gone to be replaced by parking for the commuter. Here a pannier tank, No. 3759, has charge of a number of empty hoppers, no location is given but it could very well be somewhere in the Forest of Dean where for hundreds of years coal was mined from countless pits and later exported. The result would be granite ways and later railways criss-crossing the forest.

Introduction

The name of Paul Hocquard is not one that perhaps readily comes to mind amongst the railway photographers of the 1960s - but it most definitely should be. Indeed, apart from a section of his views that appeared in 'Steam Portfolio' (the latter a compilation of the work of six photographers), published by Ian Allan in 1968, there does not appear to be much credited to him ever having appeared elsewhere.

To those of us who relish the photographer's art that is a considerable shame but hopefully we can do something within these pages to redress that balance slightly.

Unfortunately we know little of the man himself and consequently can offer no more than quote the introduction to his section within the aforementioned book.

"Which active interest came first in me, photography or railways, I cannot now remember. It was possibly the former, although it probably rekindled the earlier of my interests which, as with most of us, started when very young. I spent school holidays at Newark and my earliest railway impressions were of apple green Pacifics and Atlantics at King's Cross, with the occasional thrilling glimpse of a silver A4. It was always essential to arrive early so

(3) Mirror image, but as to where is not reported. A brace of V2s perfectly framed and also coupled together.

that time could be spent at the end of the platform wondering what would emerge tender first from the gloom of Gasworks tunnel to take us North.

"After the war while doing national service at one camp in Yorkshire near the north main line, night guard duties left me with the impression of the ultimate, but impossible railway photograph; that of a locomotive on the move at night with the firebox door open silhouetting the crew and illuminating the exhaust with shafts of crimson light.

"Eight years ago I bought a 35 mm camera and immediately I was involved in a hobby which was potentially all-absorbing; early efforts at photographing anything and everything included trains and it suddenly seemed a good idea to have my own record of something which has always interested me but which was shortly to become extinct. I took endless photographs of trains, mostly too soon or too late, out of focus or with the wrong shutter speed. But my attempts at some sort of composition, combined with improving negative and dark room techniques, started to produce a few prints, which pictorially, were acceptable. A benevolent and tolerant British Railways produced lineside passes which improved my scope but the diminishing number of steam locomotives, of increasingly grubby countenance, operating under English weather conditions, increased the odds against getting a good picture to an unacceptable level. It is amazing how the one single cloud in an otherwise cloudless sky obscures the sun just as you are about to record the picture of a lifetime! Anyway, three-quarter view type photographs as good as most of those of today were being taken 50 years ago, which says little for the potential of the modern camera.

"Little by little, while I still took conventional photographs, I also experimented with other ways of recording impressions of steam locomotives. Running sheds and stations became the biggest source of picture material. I found in such locations the necessary movement and human activity to make photography exciting, both pictorially and journalistically. Depots particularly, gave this sense of activity. Here, locomotives were coming and going, being serviced and turned, all activities which were photogenic. It was possible to predict movement and so to an extent create the picture before exposure. All this seemed much more satisfying, and at the same time recorded another aspect of steam not normally seen.

"Now, it is no longer possible to do this except on preserved railways. Everyday steam has disappeared from the English scene and out of it all, I have a few photographs of something which probably made a greater contribution to the social and commercial prosperity of this country than any other invention.

"I hope that these photographs impart some of the enjoyment I have had from my camera and the subject."

The Paul Hocquard collection arrived with the Transport Treasury by a curious route and unfortunately with no accompanying list or catalogue. Consequently, other than sometimes where the location is known (to the compiler) there is no information as to where or when. Similarly, whilst we have access to hundreds of images from which to choose (on occasions Paul would take a number of very similar views) we cannot be certain if indeed it represents all his photographs. If anyone can help in these areas both Transport Treasury and your compiler would be most grateful.

To this end I must also thank my friend the railway artist Sean Bolan who offered much constructive advice as well as being able to identify some of the more obscure subjects.

Otherwise, sit back and enjoy, this is one book that has been both a real pleasure but also a challenge - the problem not being what to put in, but more like what to leave out!

Kevin Robertson, Berkshire 2021

(4) 'De Rigueur' for the trainspotter: socks (unusually both at the same height), shirt tails hanging out and short trousers. Somewhere there will be a notebook and pencil and probably a duffle bag with jam sandwiches and if he was lucky a bottle of Tizer. The perfect ingredients for a grand day out.

Right: (5) What delights await on the platform below...... ?

The ubiquitous pannier tank could be seen throughout the Great Western and its successor the Western Region. A development of the saddle tank, the gap between the framing and the underside of the tanks allowed access to the inside motion for oiling whilst a balance pipe running across the underside of the boiler ensured there was no imbalance of weight between the two sides.

Several variations of the design existed, the earliest rebuilds from saddle tanks, whilst the most prolific were the 863 members of the 57xx type and the most numerous of any class of British steam engine. Indeed the very last of the pannier design was not introduced until 1956.

So versatile was the type that in the 1950s examples were also at work on the Western, London Midland and Southern Regions, whilst examples of the smaller 16xx design of pannier tank even worked in Scotland.

In the late 1950s, 13 were sold to London Transport and later at least six to the National Coal Board. Appropriately the final three steam engines to GWR design at work on the WR were members of the 57xx type which survived until January 1966.

Left: (6) Perhaps the thoughts of the footplate crew working hard against the gradient are on the 'The George' below...?

Right: (7) Busy pannier in the Forest of Dean and likely one of those sold out of service from British Railways to the NCB.

Left: (8) and (9) Parkend, refreshment (for the engine) and a wash for the crew. June 1965.

Above: (10) and (11) Freight crossing at Lydney; the 90° crossing here took the Severn & Wye lines from the Forest of Dean and Lydney Docks across the main GWR route from Gloucester to Newport.

(12) Paddington arrival, No. 1500 with empty stock......and in the background......

(13) Paddington departure by No. 7018 *Drysllwyn Castle*. A tragic waste when withdrawn from service after a life of less than 15 years.

Left: (14) Wet day on the Fairford branch enlivened perhaps by a game of 'hangman' on the engine tender. (The hook in the photograph is not part of the game - or for someone who perhaps did not pay the fare - and instead is waiting for a Tilley lamp to be attached.

The 22 mile Fairford branch was a truncated version of the promotors' original intention to link Witney with Cirencester by rail. A branch from Yarnton (north of Oxford) to Witney had already opened in 1861 and a separate company, the East Gloucestershire Railway opened their line from a connection at Witney on to Fairford in 1873 - but this was where it stopped. The whole was taken over by the GWR in 1890.

Right: (15) Hurried preparation of No. 6922 *Burton Hall* perhaps? Witness the smokebox ash on the step. No 6922 was new from Swindon on 19 July 1941 and ran nameless until December 1946. By October 1953 it was at Westbury but moved the following year to Oxford. At the end of the decade it had moved further north to Shrewsbury but also saw service from Tyseley. It was withdrawn from service week ending 1 May 1965 and later scrapped.

Top left: (16) Rural branch line and industry combined. Chinnor, on the way to Watlington.

Bottom left: (17) Once commonplace facility. Where stopping places existed without staff, usually a 'Halt', tickets could be obtained from the guard or from a local ticket agency.

Above: (18) Decades in the development and an enviable safety record. Western Region tubular post and from the rectangular box attached to the post, the position of this this signal was also 'repeated' in the controlling signal box.

Top right: (19) 'Stop - Look - and Listen'.

Bottom right: (20) The premier railway workshop; Swindon of course.

PASSENGERS MUST NOT CROSS THE LINE EXCEPT BY MEANS OF THE FOOTBRIDGE

Opposite: (21) Princes Risborough North displaying the (Great) Western philosophy, "...if in doubt, add a signal."

Above: (22) Next stop Bicester; but once upon a time from Princes Risborough you could also go west to Oxford (via Thame), or on the branch to Watlington. East there were trains to Aylesbury, and south to Marylebone and Paddington. Today Aylesbury is still possible as is Oxford (in 2021 that is now via Bicester). Marylebone and Paddington are also possible although for the latter a change is required.

Above: (23) On display at Snow Hill.

Opposite: (24) Working the 'fly'. The fly was the name given to the local pick-up goods services that served intermediate stations to set down and pick up wagons and odd loads; this at the time when the railway was the common carrier. Sometimes it was also a good starting point for a junior fireman in his career on the footplate.

NOTICE TO STAFF

AFF PROCEEDING TO THE OFFICES

ST NOT WALK ALONG
THE LINE

MUST USE THE AUTHORISED ROUTE
VIA THE STATION APPROACH ROAD

2261

(25) By the troughs at Goring (and one watching from the dry of the bridge). Water troughs were a feature of the GWR and Western Region and contributed towards non-stop running. Here the fireman of a 'Castle' has the scoop down as witness the overflow gushing from underneath the tender. It was a skill to lower the scoop - just the right amount - and then be able to retract it without flooding the footplate and sometimes the first coach as well. Troughs could obviously only be laid on totally level track whilst the amount of water thereabouts also meant the area was heavy on track maintenance. Might that be somebody's 'Mum' watching from the bridge?

Left: (26) 'Hall' at rest - but ready to move. No 5956 *Horsley Hall*, sat in forward gear with a wisp of steam from the front end. Somewhere under the grime was a green liveried engine.

Above: (27) 'Hall at rest' - and this time certainly not ready to move as the connecting rod is missing. The location for a WR engine in this condition is also slightly unusual as it is at the Southern shed at Eastleigh. As to why No. 6978 *Haroldstone Hall* should be under repair here is not reported. Possibly a defect which rendered a re-run to its Western Region home impractical and resulting in a running repair. No. 5956 was new in 1935 and had its final home at Oxford from October 1962, being withdrawn in March the following year.

No. 6978 saw service from November 1947, the last year of the independent Great Western Railway, and after a variety of homes, including Westbury, Laira, Old Oak Common, Southall, and Severn Tunnel Junction, spent its final four months at Ebbw Junction from March to July 1965. Neither survived into preservation.

(28) A once commonplace activity at Basingstoke for many westbound trains. No. 34036 *Westward Ho!* (believed to have been the only steam engine to ever have an exclamation mark in its name) taking water before proceeding on to Bournemouth or even Salisbury. The date has to be towards the end of steam, and sometime in 1966, as the support posts for new colour light signalling have been installed although they have yet to have the heads attached. The first vehicle with the open door is of Bulleid design.

Above: (29) Bournemouth line fast - near Micheldever. No 35024 *East Asiatic Company* with evidence of hard work from the burn marks on the smokebox door. The sleeper built and creosoted platelayers hut is another long lost feature of the steam railway.

Left: (30) Bournemouth line slow - at Micheldever, along the cess and to and from work. The advertising hoarding was for beers and ales produced by Strong's brewery at Romsey, Similar coloured hoardings were placed alongside the Bournemouth line at intervals. The engines shown also changed over the years, from original to rebuilt Bulleid types.

This page: (31) True mixed-traffic loco. No 34086 *219 Squadron,* believed to be heading north near to Micheldever.

Opposite: (32 and 33) Filthy engine but cheerful crew, No. 34018 *Axminster*. We can only hope the engine was in better condition inside than out.

Opposite: (34) Clean engine at Bournemouth Central and uniquely for the time with extended smoke deflectors. No. 34006 *Bude*.

Above: (35) Between Guildford and Redhill with a board crossing the only means of passing from one platform to the other. The swan-neck lamp on its barley-twist post has seen better days, beyond being the more modern but featureless concrete replacement.

Opposite: (36) Memorial known locally as 'Jesse's seat', in recognition of a brave railwayman and an accident back in the 19th century. It is still lovingly cared for in modern times. (Guildford to Redhill line.)

Above: (37) Traffic hold up at Reigate, but No 31826 will not not be stopping so the delay should not be for long. Fortunately too a damp day which meant although plenty of noise, there should be little or no dust from the following stone hoppers - probably eventually destined for Meldon near Okehampton.

Rowfant, between Three Bridges and East Grinstead; after 112 years of service, devoid of its railway since 1967 a casualty of Dr Beeching.

Like so many rural railways its nadir was the growth of the motor car whose flexibility allowed for individual freedom. Years earlier the Southern Railway (amongst others) had introduced some economy in working with 'pull-push' trains (others called them 'push-pull' but it was the other way around in official SR paperwork).

In this type of working a specially adapted locomotive was attached to similar specially adapted coaches with the train driver able to control the regulator (throttle) and brakes from a driving compartment at the opposite end to the engine. Meanwhile the fireman would remain on the footplate to attend to the boiler as well as adjusting the reversing gear as necessary. The driver could also operate the whistle whilst there was a basic bell-code system between the driver and fireman to cover everyday requirement, 'blow off brakes' for example. In this way a degree of economy was achieved by not having to turn the engine or run around the train at each end of the journey.

Whilst this type of working may have been thought to have ended with the demise of steam, it still persists in places in the 21st century where a locomotive is at one end of the train and a driving trailer at the other - the difference being that now the only footplate crew is the driver.

Top: (38) The train is on the point of leaving, likely the one member of staff is seen with his arm raised giving the 'Right Away' signal to indicate all the station work is complete; meanwhile the passengers are making their way to the exit.

Bottom: (39) It might be thought few changes would have affected the station over the years, but some certainly did. The colour scheme would have become green and cream compared with pre-group days, the rail-built signal is a Southern Railway (or later) addition and there is also an SR trespass notice. No doubt the paling fence would also have been replaced at least once. Most of all where once a pony and trap might have stood is now that symbol of the modern world, the motor car, seen here in the shape of a Hillman 'Minx'.

(40) Single line tablet exchange collection. This pull-push service is coming off a double line section and collecting that all-important authority to proceed. No location is given although the suggestion is Wogret Junction and the Swanage branch.

(41) Lymington Pier, one of three ways of travelling to the Isle of Wight: the others being from Southampton and Portsmouth. The branch to Lymington from Brockenhurst also gained the melancholy distinction of being 'The Last Steam Branch', and in the final days of steam was worked by BR Standard 'Class 4' tank engines and conventional rolling stock.

(42) Newport and probably Cowes train at Ryde St Johns. The loss of the railway link to Newport especially was sadly felt and whilst in 2020 there is some talk of a possibly reinstatement, there are any number of major obstacles to overcome.

(43) The terminus at Cowes likely recorded in 1964/5. Paul Hocquard took any number of excellent images on the Island, it is only a pity he was not able to record the passing of the lines to Freshwater, Bembridge, Merstone and Ventnor West.

Left: (44 and 45). Wroxall departure (for Shanklin, Sandown, Brading and Ryde). The surviving Isle of Wight railways of the 1960s were very much a microcosm of what had once been commonplace throughout Britain. No modern stock here, instead left-overs and hand-me-downs abounded. Even the finial on the starting signal was recycled from another part of the system, being of South Eastern style. Uniforms too were from a past era, the porter with the barrow especially; a long sleeve waistcoat with black sleeves.

Left: (46 and 47). The final operational steam shed on the Island at Ryde St. Johns - previously there had been a depot at Newport. Here at Ryde sunshine and shadow combine to reflect upon the one remaining class of active steam engines, the 'O2s'. Trip hazards in the form of water hydrants are also present, whilst a single member of staff stands close to the wall mounted notice boards.

Left: (48) Beauty in differing forms. At least one is admiring the other. In similar form both human and 'iron horse' had names, both now lost in the mists of time.

Right: (49) Detritus perhaps? Certainly not, and instead the works yard at Ryde where, amongst the spares and wagons perhaps awaiting attention, a newly overhauled coach has been shunted outside.

The hand crane, perhaps dating back to Victorian times, served its purpose for many decades, copious loads able to be lifted by the simple means of moving the weight box further back on its carriage. The split-spoked wheels on which the vehicle runs are another clue to its ancestry. Identifiable on the ground are vehicle springs, and at least one wheelset, the purpose of the circular items standing to the right defeating the present writer.

Top left: (50) Under the sheerlegs at Ryde. Here one end of an engine (or carriage) might be lifted for a wheelset to be removed. With limited internal covered accommodation, engines might be required to receive maintenance in the open air, hardly the ideal conditions but had it not always been thus?

Opposite bottom: (51) No. 27 *Merstone* temporarily out of service and minus its crank (drive) axle. For the present too its front end weight is being supported on packing to save excess weight being put upon the springs. The goings on outside the works also appear to be of little interest to those who stand (and sit) and wait.

Opposite vertical: (52) Signs of rationalisation at Newport. The bracket had once displayed three other signal arms - this at a time when the line to Freshwater had been open and a convoluted run-round and shunt move was needed to access the line. The service is seen departing for Cowes.

This page: (53) In Victorian times even the humble water tank might be decorated. Again Newport and where once busy engine sidings and yard space are now reduced to little more than scrub.

(54) Departure time at Waterloo - ready to give a 'shove' to the Bournemouth Belle at departure time. Silver service at one's seat or perhaps a lump of bread and cheese on the footplate?

(55) Paul was a master of capturing the moment as well - such as here at Eastleigh where the crew of this Ivatt tank are involved in replenishing the side tanks. The wagons alongside are either full of coal or ash; one commodity regularly arriving, the other regularly being removed. The monster building behind is the enginemen's lobby as well as the shed offices and originally dormitories, although how anyone might have been expected to sleep with the noise of a busy shed immediately outside is anyone's guess. The signal was not to determine a route but was used to test eyesight.

Left and opposite: (56-58) Photography as an art can take on many forms; some saying the perfectly composed 'three-quarter' view with the engine rods 'down', a wisp of steam - a clean engine of course - and a few clouds to give depth to the view is the ideal image. Indeed this was the style of photograph so favoured in pre-war days. Later came those who were prepared to experiment, and whilst we are deliberately not mentioning names, the reader will, I am sure, be familiar with the more 'experimental' photographers.

Paul Hocquard had an eye for an image that most of us mere mortals could not comprehend. Mentioning one name in general terms, the late Maurice Earley was known to sometimes visit a potential photographic location to 'size it up', looking for the ideal position considering the time of day and consequent light available. He should also take the credit for running railway photography classes where he might share his skills and so encourage others who were similarly keen to try and obtain the perfect shot.

This is where Paul and others of his type were different. Yes, sometimes we do see the three-quarter view, but it will always be with something else included, this to add depth, contrast, in effect to frame the subject. In similar fashion how many ever considered including the everyday tasks involving in running the railway, be that in the running shed, on the platform or in the signal box? This book contains examples of all.

In this spread we have three views of Nine Elms. Do they need much in the way of words? Not really. But don't just glimpse, study each in detail. On the left the engine in the shed and another outside, the latter receiving some sort of attention. Note the hand trolley and coiled hose, the trolley of the type equally at home on a platform, perhaps it had been 'borrowed'.

On the right the men, the behind the scenes workers, those who kept the engines running, none in the first flower of youth and yet continuing to undertake a dirty, heavy task for little reward. Nothing to do with the steam railway was light in weight. The late 1950s and 1960s were not a good time for BR Younger men were leaving for better paid work in cleaner environments, and BR just could not compete.

Above: (59) Starting them young (at Waterloo), is he still a train spotter perhaps…..?

Opposite: (60) Bulleid power at Bournemouth.

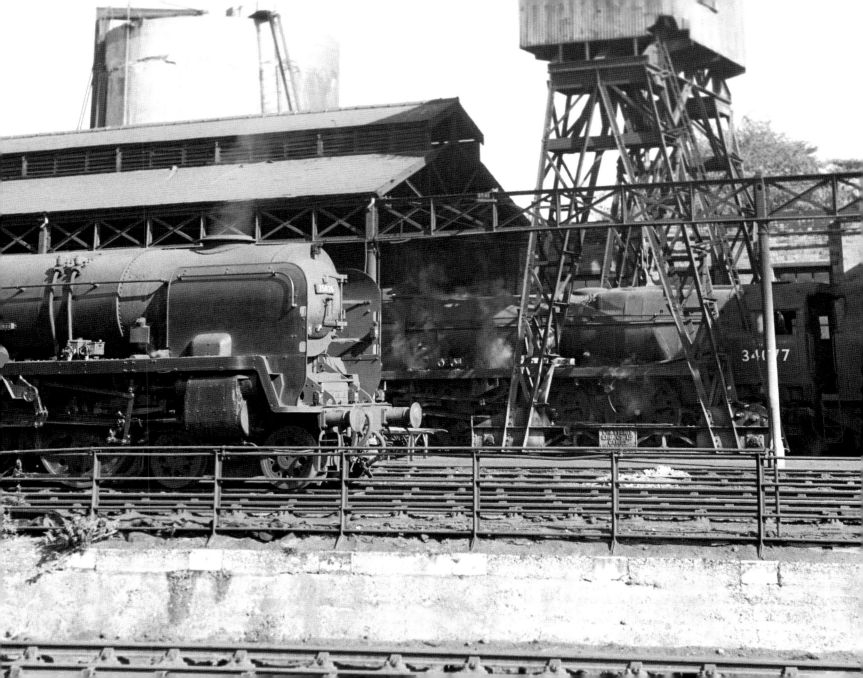

(61) At Bournemouth Central's long down platform, No. 34048 *Crediton* has just arrived with a service from Waterloo - the number '466' on the headcode refers to the loco duty. New from Brighton in November 1946 as 21C148, the engine was renumbered in more conventional form in September 1948. Just over ten years later it was rebuilt as seen and survived until March 1966. Soon after, Bournemouth station would be remodelled in connection with forthcoming electrification, the two centre tracks permanently removed.

(62) And speaking of electrification, alongside this came an extension of multiple aspect colour light signalling, a gantry for which can be seen in the background. In its last months, perhaps even weeks or even days of operational service, this is an example of the low-pressure pneumatic signalling that existed in the Basingstoke area until late 1966. The lower quadrant arms had seen service since LSWR days and were activated by track circuit.

(63) Water softening at Brighton shed. The chute was to allow sludge to be removed into a waiting wagon. On the wooden bodied wagon is inscribed 'Loco Coal, one journey only', perhaps like the steam engine, it too was nearing the end. Strange to relate that despite being in the midst of electrified lines, steam locomotives operated west from Brighton well into the 1960s, their role being to provide power on the through trains to Plymouth and the Western Region.

(64) A particular favourite is this view of Bath Green Park. The local 'moggie' may well have been on the payroll with the task of keeping down the rodent population. It seems totally unfazed by the goings on, neither passengers, trains nor the abundant smell of lamp oil behind is a problem. On the left between the tracks is a ground frame to change the points for the engine release crossover.

Left: (65), right: (66 and 67). Inside the signal box and an ideal location for the photographer's art. This is the interior of Binegar signal box on the Somerset & Dorset line south from Bath and in general terms probably changed little since its original opening. The frame however is a relatively modern fitment by Westinghouse with both conventional and push-pull levers.

Most of the levers are seen on the left; this is their 'normal' position. Those at the end are reversed and are almost certainly signals that have been pulled 'off' for the approaching train. The position of the levers in the frame was a mirror of the position of the actual track and signal layout with up and down line signals at the ends of the frame and the points (turnouts) within the station area placed in the middle of the frame.

The levers standing midway are those of the push-pull type (not to be confused with 'push-pull' trains). These levers could operate two items dependent upon whether they were pushed forward or pulled back; it was a way of economising in the number of levers and was a common feature with some companies. Each lever was also painted - colour coded - as to its purpose. Red for stop signals, yellow for distant signals, black for points, and blue for point locks. The light painted levers here are not yellow - distant signals would be at each end of the frame - and are instead painted white, meaning they are spare levers; either permanent spares incorporated into the frame in case the layout were expanded and extra levers were required, or as in this case, where equipment has been taken out of use.

On the block shelf are the actual instruments with which the signalman would communicate with his opposite number at the signal boxes either side. Signalling instruments were operated on the simple premise of 'yes' or no' ('Line Clear' or 'Line Blocked'), in that way there was never any doubt as to what was occurring.

In the view opposite we see the actual duty man returning the levers to normal after the passage of a train, he is also using his duster which not only allowed the polished top of the lever to slide easily through the hands but also prevented smears on the top of the lever. Signalmen were proud men. It was a solitary existence and most would devote a considerable amount of time to keeping their work environment as clean as possible. This included the telephone, desk, lamps and the wonderful 'SCR' bell ('Somerset Central Railway'). In olden days the latter would have been rung to signify an approaching train to passengers and station staff.

The role of the signalman was a responsible job and each would have to be conversant with the signalling regulations as well as the working and train service of his particular box. Regular refresher examinations took place to ensure competence was maintained.

Another task was to observe the train as it passed; no signs of alarm being given, door handles 'turned', no unusual noises, and most importantly that a tail lamp was present on the last vehicle. All would also be recorded in the Train Register book.

Left: (68) Binegar again and a local service awaiting departure. Sadly the S&D line was a casualty of the 1960s, through communication between Bath and Bournemouth now involving a roundabout rail journey with at least one change or alternatively a slow road journey on a route which is ever congested.

Right: (69) Sutton Coldfield, for the moment at least resting quietly in the sunshine.

(69) Once considered the very latest and most desirable but now out of fashion and the least wanted. Coaches of various eras redundant and stored at Wolverton (or is it Verney Junction?). How many 'bums on seats' might have been carried, how many journeys made and to where? Work, pleasure, enforced separation: been there, done that, seen it all and now superseeded, old-fashined, awaiting the very last journey - to the scrappers.

Left: (70) The products of Mr Stanier - 1. No. 42611 is one of a class of 206 2-6-4T engines built at Derby and by North British between 1934 and 1943. The design was one of two cylinders and was based on the earlier LMS 3-cylinder type. Seen from above, the tank water fillers are apparent as are the various fire-irons resting on the left hand tank top.

At the front end of the tanks the British Railways electrification flash warnings, the latter red on white and intended to remind staff of the dangers of overhead wires if they are working in such an area. Two other features to mention are the oval buffers and the degree of horizontal movement that is available to the coupling. Both these features were repeated at the rear and were designed to allow the engine to push vehicles around sharp curves without encountering buffer-lock; which is where one buffer rides around (or even above) another so creating the conditions for derailment.

Right: (71) The products of Mr Stanier - 2. One of his ubiquitous 'Class 5' tender engines also known as 'Black 5s'. This was the go anywhere, do anything steam engine on the LMS, with no less than 842 built and able to be seen anywhere from the north of Scotland and as far south as Bournemouth. There were variants of course including some with Caprotti valve gear and others with outside Stephenson link motion. Here No. 44704 is the object of admiration at Perth, also its home depot, or could it be slight trepidation from the youngest generation?

Above: (72), opposite (73 and 74).'Replenishing the beast' with coal and water, and an example of the very rudimentary facilities that were sometimes all that was available for maintenance at the running sheds. At least for the first named a modern day coal-hopper is available but with it came voluminous quantities of dust.

Left: (75) Deep in thought perhaps? The engine another LMS design, the class acquiring the rather unkind nicknames of 'Doodlebugs' or 'Flying Pigs' but as to why is not certain.

Right: (76) 'We shall not be hurried....' At Carmont, north of Dundee, on the way to Aberdeen. It was at places such as this where time had almost stood still for generations, true the engines and trains that passed may have altered but otherwise life went on as it always had - there was even a station here to serve the rural community. That is until one day in May 1964 when after a life of 109 years, 'London' decreed it was no longer commercially viable, and whilst trains may still pass, it is a long time since one stopped here. (But the cows continue to cross twice a day.)

(Left: (77) Right: (78) Stragglers at Carmont.

(79) How many might have trodden a similar path and viewed what in the past: Midland 4-4-0s, Johnson 'Spinners' and before that perhaps even Cramptons... .

Above: (80) and Right (81) Unofficial visit no doubt, perhaps after school or a weekend. From ground level it is no wonder the smallest of the group appears visually intimidated; as well he might, 83 tons plus tender - v- perhaps three stone... . No. 46158 *The Loyal Regiment* ignores it all; a passing phase of interest or the early years of lifelong interest? Would similar be allowed today? Never, 'health and safety' would see to that and probably right as well – from one who speaks from experience of the steam era.... .

(82) It can only be on one of the steep gradients in the North West - Beattock perhaps? (Oh for a list of images!) A 'Black 5' and two Class 4 tanks seemingly battle to take a train of just 20 wagons including van up the grade. It is possible the train engine may not be doing very well; lots of smoke and seemingly a limited blast. Pity the poor guard as well, for him the noise must have been considerable.

(83) Occupation crossing, somewhere to get close - and at the same time legal. Another grimy 'Black 5', this one No. 44858, new in 1934 and which ended its life from Carlisle Kingmoor at the end of December 1967, less than six months from the end of all steam. Is the fireman just acknowledging the youngsters or even warning them of the approaching DMU?

(84) Location puzzle - someone will know it as their local station. LMR or ER? Perhaps the latter due to the presence of the very tall concrete post signal. 'Barrows, bicycle, and brick', the latter nearest the barrows perhaps even a surviving air-raid shelter. The coach is clearly in Engineer's use but both the wording on the side and that on the end of the signal box in the distance are just too indistinct to be read with complete certainty.

(85) Close examination. (Note, the supposed addition to the top of the cab is in fact the mast of a lighting pole behind!) No. 61319 is a North British Locomotive Co built (one of 50 from this manufacturer) 'B1' 4-6-0 dating from May 1948 allocated new to Newcastle Borough Gardens. A decade later it moved to Wakefield and a few months on to Darlington before a final move to York (North) the following year, 1959. Here it would remain until the end of its working life in December 1966. Two months later it was summarily dispatched by Messrs A Draper at Hull. During what was a short 18+ year life, the engine carried six different boilers and also made 14 works visits, two of these, in 1949 and 1954, following collision damage although detail of the actual incidents are not given.

Introduced originally in 1942, the type were the LNER equivalent of the LMS 'Black 5' and as might then be expected they were also destined to be numerous. Indeed a total of 410 were built between 1942 and 1952 although one, No. 61057, was written off in an accident at Witham Junction in 1950 and subsequently scrapped so meaning the maximum number on the books was destined to be 409.

Several of the type were also named, the first 41 after antelopes but with one exception, *Ralph Anderson* who was a politician who served in Winston Churchill's wartime cabinet. A further 17 were named after prominent figures connected with the Conservative party and some LNER directors. One of antelope names used was Bongo, so it was not surprising that the whole class were quickly known by the same nickname.

In service the class could be seen from one end of the LNER to the next, equally at home working from King's Cross, Liverpool Street, into East Anglia, and in the north. One issue they had was that they quickly developed a reputation for harsh riding, something LNER men had not been used to with Gresley designs.

Clearly No. 61319 (un-named) is under close scrutiny here, whether it was stored at the time or just awaiting its next duty we cannot say, what is certain is that the class total started to be depleted from 1961 onwards, one example going in 1961 but 120 the following year. No. 61319 was one of 64 to cease work in 1964 with the final 27 taken out of service in 1967. Two of the class, Nos. No. 61264 and 61305 were saved from the breakers.

This page: (86 and 87) Works and shed attention, including for a special 'A4', No. 60007 *Sir Nigel Gresley*.

Opposite page: (88 and 89) A3's at rest; the look of the type with the addition of the German type half deflector is open to debate.

Left: (90) Last minute instructions perhaps to the driver, or a problem perhaps with the injector? Meanwhile the fireman takes the advantage to water the coal - intended to keep the dust down - which may indicate the engine is shortly to undertake some tender first running, assuming it is not declared a failure that is! No. 60532 was named *Blue Peter* (another example of the LNER's policy of naming engines after winning race-horses) and as such also achieved a connection with the BBC children's programme of the same name. Indeed, contributions from young viewers helped towards its later restoration to working order.

Withdrawn from service in 1966 the engine entered preservation but suffered a major failure at Durham in 1994 with water carried over to the regulator valve, jamming this open, and a consequent rush of steam to the cylinders. In attempting to control what was now a major slip the driver moved to turn the reversing gear but this flew forward resulting in injury to him. The spin then accelerated until the driving wheels reached a rotational speed of 140mph before the cylinder covers blew off and the motion simply disintegrated. The driving wheels were similarly damaged. Repairs took 18 months to complete but No. 60532 did work again although like every other preserved steam engine is also subject to other repairs and inspections and at the time of writing is undergoing overhaul.

Right: (91) A task undertaken thousands of times and yet rarely recorded, 'tying the engine on to the train'. Invariably the role of the fireman, the work will include: the coupling itself, the vacuum pipes, the steam-heat hose (if appropriate) and finally removal of the engine head/ tail lamp.

Above: (92) A clean 'WD' 2-8-0, now that is a rarity.

Opposite: (93 and 94) Contrasting front end designs, No. 60034 *Lord Faringdon* at Perth, when working the Aberdeen - Glasgow (Buchanan Street) service, and No. 60100 *Spearmint*.

Left: (95) *Lord Faringdon* again, this time with 'cod's mouth' open and smokebox (or is it tube?) cleaning taking place. The remnants of the white painted buffers are indicative of recent railtour working.

Above: (96) Steam and Scammell Scarab. The steam engine, another 'A4', this one No. 60031 *Golden Plover,* is the steam example - the carrier is of passengers and goods and shown here in its last days, with yellow cab stripe indicating it must not work under electrified lines. The Scammell Scarab is an example of thousands of similar small articulated vehicles used by the railway companies and then British Railways at a time when parcels traffic was a major part of railway business. It is seen in the yellow livery of National Carriers complete with emblem that in many ways was similar to the BR 'double arrow'.

(97) Non-public passenger rolling stock. Eastern Region - signified by the 'E' prefix and suffix, Royal Mail storage/sorting van. The offset corridor connection was also for security purposes meaning it was not compatible with a centre connection and consequently was secure from the rest of the train. Note too the shape of the buffer heads. Clearly dating from LNER days, it runs on Gresley type bogies.

(98) Engineer's or officer's inspection saloon and likely dating back to North Eastern Railway days. The bulbous side extension allowed for a forward and reverse look out, similar to that provided by a guard's ducket on some conventional passenger rolling stock. There were several such vehicles on all railways, used as the name implies, on tours of inspection sometimes at director level and other times for engineers and the like.

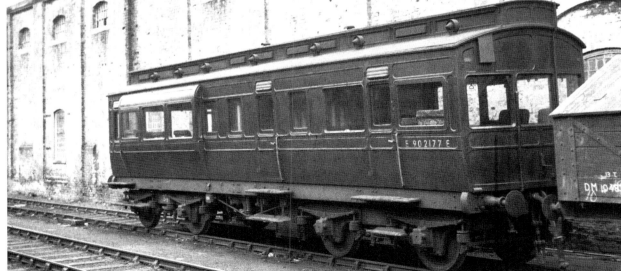

This page: (99 and 100) In 1967, In 1967, *Charlie,* BR's last railway shunting horse, was withdrawn. Fortunately, unlike the iron horses he had worked alongside, when the time came *Charlie* was retired to a Somerset farm. *Charlie's* domain had been the sidings at Newmarket where under the command of his railway master, Lawrence Kelly, he would move the horse boxes as required. Charlie was indeed the last of thousands of animals once used in a similar role up and down the country - sometimes a coal merchant's horse might even be 'borrowed' as necessary. Whilst horses can sometimes be wary about unusual surfaces, this one was not and would happily step over the running rails and walk on sleepers or ballast as necessary. As well as shunting work, horses had also been a regular feature of railway collections and deliveries from station goods yards.

Opposite: (101) Another sight now consigned to history is that of the Pooley van. This company were one of those responsible for the regular maintenance and accuracy of weighbridges and smaller weighscales used on railway premises. Amongst the equipment carried were 'master-weights' which were used to assess the accuracy of the scales with adjustments made when necessary.

(102) Just one example of what had once been a common sight, namely the variety in the make-up of trains in the steam and even the early diesel era. On this service the first four vehicles are all totally different and there is every reason to believe the remainder of the train was just as varied.

(103) 'OK to move', 'Clear of turntable', or 'We like this!'. Steam and diesel, perhaps not in absolute harmony. The diesel era was meant to portray a clean new image for the railway - unlike our friend's jacket and trousers that is! Maintaining the new traction in a steam environment was also not ideal and who could blame the men for wanting change as well; hard, dirty work on steam, or the same task performed in comfort on the diesel.

(104) Today's railway station is a clean, bright place, often peppered with retail outlets and a far cry from the 1950s and even much of the 1960s. To achieve this change there were obviously casualties, one example being memorials such as 'Wimbledon Nell' whose role was to collect funds for the LSWR orphanage in both life, and later in death.